LE CORDON BLEU

HOME COLLECTION

·BREAD·

contents

recipe ratings ✸ *easy* ✸✸ *a little more care needed* ✸✸✸ *more care needed*

White bread

Baking fresh bread is one of the most pleasurable ways of feeding family and friends and is also a relaxing way to spend an afternoon. Start with this classic white loaf.

Preparation time **20 minutes + proving**
   (about 4 hours 30 minutes)
Total cooking time **40 minutes**
Makes **1 x 750 g (1¹/₂ lb) loaf**

30 g (1 oz) fresh yeast or 1 tablespoon dried yeast
1 tablespoon sugar
500 g (1 lb) white bread flour
1 teaspoon salt
30 g (1 oz) butter, softened
milk, to glaze

1 Prepare the yeast with 300 ml (10 fl oz) water and the sugar following the method in the Chef's techniques on page 62.

2 Sieve the flour and salt into a large mixing bowl and make a well in the centre. Add the yeast mixture and butter to the well and gradually bring the mixture together with your hands, or use an electric mixer fitted with a dough hook on slow speed, until a rough dough is formed. Turn the dough out onto a lightly floured work surface and knead for about 10 minutes, or until smooth and elastic (see Chef's techniques, page 62). Alternatively, knead in an electric mixer on medium speed for about 5 minutes.

3 Return the dough to a clean, lightly oiled bowl and turn once to coat the surface in oil. Cover with a clean, damp tea towel and allow to prove at room temperature until doubled in size (the proving time will depend on the temperature of your kitchen).

4 Turn the dough out onto a lightly floured work surface and knead gently for 2–3 minutes until smooth. Roll into a 25 x 45 cm (10 x 18 inch) rectangle and shape the loaf by rolling up tightly into a sausage shape (see Chef's techniques, page 63).

5 Butter a baking tray and lift the bread onto the tray, seam-side-down. Use a very sharp knife to cut diagonal slashes in a crisscross pattern on the top of the loaf (see Chef's techniques, page 63). Cover with a damp tea towel and allow to rise again until nearly doubled in size. Towards the end of this time, preheat the oven to hot 210°C (415°F/Gas 6–7).

6 Brush the proved loaf with the milk and bake for 35–40 minutes, or until golden brown and hollow sounding when tapped on the base. Remove from the tray and cool on a wire rack.

Chef's tip To make rolls, divide the dough into sixteen equal-sized pieces and roll each piece on a lightly floured work surface in the hollow of your hand until it forms a round and smooth ball. Bake for 15–20 minutes.

Baguette

Professional bakers use a special flour for baguettes that is not readily available to the home cook, but using a mixture of bread and plain flours produces an excellent version of this classic French bread.

*Preparation time **45 minutes + proving**
(about 3 hours 30 minutes)*
*Total cooking time **25 minutes***
Makes 4 x 350 g (11 oz) loaves

30 g (1 oz) fresh yeast or 1 tablespoon dried yeast
650 g (1 lb 5 oz) white bread flour
350 g (11 oz) plain flour
10 g (1/4 oz) salt

1 Prepare the yeast with 600 ml (20 fl oz) water following the method in the Chef's techniques on page 62.
2 Sieve the flours and salt into a large mixing bowl and make a well in the centre. Add the yeast mixture to the well and gradually bring the mixture together with your hands, or use an electric mixer fitted with a dough hook on slow speed, until a rough dough is formed. Turn the dough out onto a lightly floured work surface and knead for about 10 minutes, or until smooth and elastic (see Chef's techniques, page 62). Alternatively, knead in an electric mixer on medium speed for about 5 minutes.

3 Return the dough to a clean, lightly oiled bowl and turn once to coat the surface in oil. Cover with a clean, damp tea towel and allow to prove at room temperature until doubled in size (the proving time will depend on the temperature of your kitchen).
4 Turn the dough out onto a lightly floured work surface and knead gently for 2–3 minutes until smooth. Divide the dough into four pieces, shape each piece into a rough rectangle about 30 cm (12 inches) long and roll tightly into long baguette shapes.
5 Sprinkle flour over a baking tray and lift the bread onto the tray, allowing plenty of space between each loaf. Spray the loaves with a fine mist of water and sprinkle with flour. Use a very sharp knife to cut five diagonal slashes on the top of each loaf, to a depth of about 5 mm (1/4 inch) (see Chef's techniques, page 63). Cover with a damp tea towel and allow to rise again until nearly doubled in size. Towards the end of this time, preheat the oven to hot 220°C (425°F/Gas 7).
6 Bake the proved baguettes for 20–25 minutes, or until golden brown, crisp and hollow sounding when tapped on the base. Remove from the tray and cool on a wire rack.

Ciabatta

Ciabatta is Italian for 'slipper', a good description of this rustic oval-shaped Italian loaf. The olive oil gives the bread its crusty texture and delicate handling with little knocking back after rising creates the holes.

Preparation time **30 minutes + proving**
   (about 4–5 hours)
Total cooking time **40 minutes**
Makes 2 x 650 g (1 lb 5 oz) loaves

30 g (1 oz) fresh yeast or 1 tablespoon dried yeast
680 g (1 lb 6 oz) white bread flour
140 ml (4¹/2 fl oz) extra virgin olive oil
3 teaspoons salt

1 Prepare the yeast with 440 ml (14 fl oz) water following the method in the Chef's techniques on page 62.

2 Sieve half the flour into a large mixing bowl and make a well in the centre. Add the yeast mixture and olive oil to the well. Using your hand with fingers slightly apart, gradually draw the flour into the liquid. Continue until all the flour has been incorporated and a loose batter has formed, then beat for 5 minutes with your hand to develop the elasticity of the dough. Clean the sides of the bowl with a scraper, cover with a clean, damp tea towel and allow to prove at room temperature until doubled in size (the proving time will depend on the temperature of your kitchen).

3 Add the remaining flour and salt to the risen dough and beat with a wooden spoon to mix. Scrape down the sides of the bowl, cover with a damp tea towel and allow to rise again until nearly doubled in size

4 Divide the dough, which will be very soft, in half, handling gently to retain its characteristic holey texture.

5 Lightly butter and flour two baking trays and lift the bread onto the trays. With damp hands, gently shape each piece into a rough rectangle about 2.5 cm (1 inch) thick. Spray the loaves with a fine mist of water and sprinkle heavily with flour. Cover with a damp tea towel and allow to prove again until nearly doubled in size. Towards the end of this time, preheat the oven to very hot 230°C (450°F/Gas 8).

6 Bake the proved ciabattas for 35–40 minutes, or until pale golden and hollow sounding when tapped on the base. Remove from the tray and cool on a wire rack. Leave for 20 minutes before serving.

Chef's tips To make olive ciabatta, add 200 g (6¹/2 oz) roughly chopped pitted olives to the dough with the flour and salt in Step 3.

Alternatively, add the same amount of chopped sun-dried tomatoes or two very thinly sliced large onions, sautéed first in a little butter until soft but not coloured.

Focaccia

This soft Italian bread is traditionally filled or topped with delicious ingredients—here sea salt, herbs and olives. Serve with a simple tomato salad and some Parmesan for lunch.

Preparation time **35 minutes + proving**
   (about 3 hours)
Total cooking time **20 minutes**
Makes 2 x 800 g (1 lb 10 oz) loaves

30 g (1 oz) fresh yeast or 1 tablespoon dried yeast
900 g (1 lb 14 oz) white bread flour
1 teaspoon salt
leaves from 4 sprigs of fresh rosemary, chopped
6 cloves garlic, finely chopped
5 eggs, beaten
155 ml (5 fl oz) olive oil
125 g (4 oz) spicy black olives, pitted
2 tablespoons chopped mixed fresh herbs
2 teaspoons sea salt

1 Prepare the yeast with 300 ml (10 fl oz) water following the method in the Chef's techniques on page 62.

2 Sieve the flour and salt into a large mixing bowl, stir in the rosemary and garlic and make a well in the centre. Add the yeast mixture to the well, followed by the eggs and half the oil. Using your hand with fingers slightly apart, gradually draw the flour into the liquid. Continue until all the flour has been incorporated and a rough dough is formed. Turn the dough out onto a lightly floured work surface and knead for about 10 minutes, or until smooth and elastic (see Chef's techniques, page 62).

3 Return the dough to a clean, lightly oiled bowl and turn once to coat the surface in oil. Cover with a clean, damp tea towel and allow to prove at room temperature until doubled in size (the proving time will depend on the temperature of your kitchen).

4 Turn the dough out onto a lightly floured work surface and knead gently for 2–3 minutes until smooth. Divide the dough in half and roll out into rectangles to fit two lightly floured 20 x 25 cm (8 x 10 inch) baking trays. Cover with a damp tea towel and allow to rise again until nearly doubled in size. Towards the end of this time, preheat the oven to very hot 230°C (450°F/Gas 8).

5 With your fingers, make deep holes over the surface of the proved dough at irregular intervals. Push the olives into the holes and brush the surface of the bread liberally with most of the remaining olive oil. Sprinkle with the mixed herbs and sea salt.

6 Bake for 20 minutes, or until golden brown. As soon as the focaccia comes out of the oven, brush again with the remaining olive oil. Best eaten immediately.

Granary bread

Granary flour purchased ready-mixed with a whole range of grains is added here to thick, honey-like malt to makes a superb, easy loaf.

*Preparation time **25 minutes + proving**
(about 2 hours 30 minutes)*
*Total cooking time **35 minutes***
Makes 1 x 1 kg (2 lb) loaf

☼

**40 g (1¼ oz) fresh yeast or 1¼ tablespoons
dried yeast**
500 g (1 lb) malted grain or granary flour
1 teaspoon salt
1 teaspoon sugar
30 g (1 oz) butter
2 teaspoons liquid malt
beaten egg, to glaze

1 Prepare the yeast with 300 ml (10 fl oz) water following the method in the Chef's techniques on page 62.
2 Place the flour, salt and sugar into a large mixing bowl, stir to mix and make a well in the centre. Melt the butter in a small pan over low heat, add the liquid malt and stir until smooth. Add this to the well with the yeast mixture. Using your hand with fingers slightly apart, gradually draw the flour into the liquid. Continue until all the flour has been incorporated and a soft dough is formed. Turn the dough out onto a lightly floured work surface and knead for about 10 minutes, or until smooth and elastic (see Chef's techniques, page 62).
3 Return the dough to a clean, lightly oiled bowl and turn once to coat the surface in oil. Cover with a clean, damp tea towel and allow to prove at room temperature until doubled in size (the proving time will depend on the temperature of your kitchen).
4 Butter and flour a 20 x 9 x 9 cm (8 x 3½ x 3½ inch) 1 kg (2 lb) loaf tin, tapping out any excess flour. Turn the dough out onto a lightly floured work surface and knead for 1 minute. Using your hands, pat out to a square slightly longer than the tin and spray with a fine mist of water. Shape the loaf by rolling up tightly into a sausage shape (see Chef's techniques, page 63), then lift the bread into the prepared tin, seam-side-down. Cover with a damp tea towel and allow to rise again until nearly doubled in size. Towards the end of this time, preheat the oven to very hot 230°C (450°F/Gas 8).
5 Brush the proved loaf with egg and use a very sharp knife to make a slash down the length of the loaf (see Chef's techniques, page 63). Bake for 30–35 minutes, or until golden brown and hollow sounding when tapped on the base. Remove from the tray and cool on a wire rack.

Chef's tip Liquid malt is available from health food shops and has the same consistency as honey.

Petits pains au lait

These small rolls are made with an enriched bread dough and milk for a soft texture and golden crust.
They are great as dinner rolls to accompany a French meal.

Preparation time **40 minutes + proving**
   (about 3–4 hours)
Total cooking time **15 minutes**
Makes 16 dinner rolls

☀

30 g (1 oz) fresh yeast or 1 tablespoon dried yeast
1 tablespoon sugar
500 g (1 lb) white bread flour
1 teaspoon salt
30 g (1 oz) milk powder
30 g (1 oz) butter, softened
milk, to glaze
3 tablespoons nibbed sugar, to decorate (optional)

1 Prepare the yeast with 300 ml (10 fl oz) water and the sugar following the method in the Chef's techniques on page 62.

2 Sieve the flour, salt and milk powder into a large mixing bowl and make a well in the centre. Add the yeast mixture and butter to the well and gradually bring the mixture together with your hands, or use an electric mixer fitted with a dough hook on slow speed, until a rough dough is formed. Turn the dough out onto a lightly floured work surface and knead for about 10 minutes, or until smooth and elastic (see Chef's

techniques, page 62). Alternatively, knead in an electric mixer on medium speed for about 5 minutes.

3 Return the dough to a clean, lightly oiled bowl and turn once to coat the surface in oil. Cover with a clean, damp tea towel and allow to prove at room temperature until doubled in size (the proving time will depend on the temperature of your kitchen).

4 Turn the dough out onto a lightly floured work surface and knead gently for 2–3 minutes until smooth. Divide the dough into sixteen equal-sized pieces. Roll each piece on a lightly floured work surface in the hollow of your hand until it forms a round and smooth ball, then flatten slightly and roll into miniature loaves with elongated ends.

5 Butter two baking trays and lift the rolls onto the trays, allowing plenty of space between each one. Cover with a damp tea towel and allow to rise again until nearly doubled in size. Towards the end of this time, preheat the oven to hot 210°C (415°F/Gas 6–7).

6 Brush the proved rolls with the milk and, using scissors, snip into the tops of the rolls along their length to a depth of about 1 cm (1/2 inch) (see Chef's techniques, page 63). Sprinkle with the nibbed sugar, if using, and bake for 10–12 minutes, or until golden brown and hollow sounding when tapped on the base. Remove from the tray and cool on a wire rack.

Grissini

Thin, crispy sticks of Italian bread that are easy and fun to make. With these, it's all in the hand action—even, smooth rolling of the sticks means less knobbly results.

Preparation time **55 minutes + proving time**
  (about 2 hours 45 minutes)
Total cooking time **15 minutes**
Makes 45 grissini

15 g (¹/₂ oz) fresh yeast or 2 teaspoons dried yeast
450 g (14¹/₄ oz) brown or white bread flour
2 teaspoons sea salt
2 tablespoons oil
beaten egg, to glaze
2 tablespoons poppy seeds
1 teaspoon Marmite or Vegemite

1 Prepare the yeast with 125 ml (4 fl oz) water following the method in the Chef's techniques on page 62.
2 Sponge the dough by sieving the flour into a large mixing bowl, adding the salt and following the method in the Chef's techniques on page 63. Add 125 ml (4 fl oz) lukewarm water and the oil to the well after the yeast has risen and stir to form a soft dough. Turn the dough out onto a lightly floured work surface and knead for about 10 minutes, or until smooth and elastic (see Chef's techniques, page 62). Alternatively, knead in an electric mixer on medium speed for about 5 minutes.

3 Return the dough to a clean, lightly oiled bowl and turn once to coat the surface in oil. Cover with a clean, damp tea towel and allow to prove at room temperature until doubled in size (the proving time will depend on the temperature of your kitchen). Preheat the oven to very hot 230°C (450°F/Gas 8).
4 Turn the dough out onto a work surface and knead gently for 2–3 minutes until smooth (it is easier not to flour the work surface when shaping grissini. If the dough does stick, spray with a fine mist of water). Roll out into a thin 40 x 20 cm (16 x 8 inch) rectangle. Cut in half lengthways, then into strips about 1 cm (¹/₂ inch) wide. Roll the strips of dough under your hands until they are even and about 25 cm (10 inches) long. Butter two baking trays and lift the grissini onto the trays.
5 Brush half the grissini with the beaten egg and sprinkle with the poppy seeds. Mix together the Marmite or Vegemite and 2 tablespoons of boiling water and brush over the remaining grissini. Bake for about 10–15 minutes, turning halfway through. Remove from the trays and cool on a wire rack. Store in an airtight container for up to a week.

Chef's tip Grissini are great with thin strips of Parma ham wrapped around them or served with spicy or creamy dips.

Hazelnut bread

*This nutty white loaf can be eaten toasted or plain. Spread with creamy French butter
and whole fruit conserves for a relaxing weekend breakfast.*

Preparation time **10 minutes + proving
(about 3 hours 30 minutes)**
Total cooking time **50 minutes**
Makes 1 x 850 g (1 lb 12 oz) loaf

30 g (1 oz) fresh yeast or 1 tablespoon dried yeast
¹/₂ teaspoon sugar
500 g (1 lb) white bread flour
15 g (¹/₂ oz) milk powder
¹/₂ teaspoon salt
150 g (5 oz) skinned hazelnuts, roughly chopped
milk, to glaze

1 Prepare the yeast with 300 ml (10 fl oz) water and
the sugar following the method in the Chef's techniques
on page 62.
2 Sieve the flour, milk powder and salt into a large
mixing bowl and make a well in the centre. Add the
yeast mixture to the well and gradually bring the
mixture together with your hands, or use an electric
mixer fitted with a dough hook on slow speed, until a
rough dough is formed. Turn the dough out onto a
lightly floured work surface and knead for about
10 minutes, or until smooth and elastic (see Chef's

techniques, page 62). Alternatively, knead in an electric
mixer on medium speed for about 5 minutes.
3 Return the dough to a clean, lightly oiled bowl and
turn once to coat the surface in oil. Cover with a clean,
damp tea towel and allow to prove at room temperature
until doubled in size (the proving time will depend on
the temperature of your kitchen).
4 Turn the dough out onto a lightly floured work
surface and knead gently for 2–3 minutes until smooth.
Add the hazelnuts and knead until they are evenly
distributed through the dough. Take one third of the
dough and shape on a lightly floured surface into a
smooth ball. Do the same for the remaining piece.
Butter a baking tray and lift the larger ball onto the tray,
flatten slightly, brush the top with water and place the
smaller ball on top. Using the handle of a wooden
spoon, press a deep hole through the centre of both
balls, flattening them slightly. Cover with a damp tea
towel and allow to rise again until nearly doubled in
size. Towards the end of this time, preheat the oven to
hot 210°C (415°F/Gas 6–7).
5 Brush the proved loaf with the milk and bake for
45–50 minutes, or until golden brown and hollow
sounding when tapped on the base. Remove from the
tray and cool on a wire rack.

*Damper is really good.
Carful not to under or over
Cut the center cross*

Damper

*Damper was traditionally an Australian campfire
bread. Nowadays it is a useful quick bread using
self-raising flour as a raising agent instead of yeast.*

Preparation time **15 minutes**
Total cooking time **45 minutes**
Makes 1 x 800 g (1 lb 10 oz) loaf

375 g (12 oz) self-raising flour
155 g (5 oz) wholemeal flour
1 teaspoon salt
30 g (1 oz) butter, melted
410 ml (13 fl oz) milk
milk, to glaze

1 Preheat the oven to hot 210°C (415°F/Gas 6–7).
Sieve the flours and salt into a large mixing bowl,
returning any husks in the sieve to the flour in the bowl,
and make a well in the centre.
2 Mix the melted butter and milk together and pour
about three-quarters into the well. Using a round-
bladed knife, quickly and lightly mix the liquid into the
flour with a cutting action. Add as much of the
remaining milk mixture as needed to produce a rough,
slightly sticky ball that leaves the sides of the bowl.
3 Turn the dough out onto a lightly floured work
surface and knead for 1 minute, or until it forms a
smooth ball.
4 Butter a baking tray, lift the bread onto the tray and
flatten slightly. Use a very sharp knife to slash a cross in
the top of the bread to a depth of 2 cm (3/4 inch) (see
Chef's techniques, page 63).
5 Brush the damper with the milk and sprinkle with
some extra wholemeal flour. Bake for 15 minutes, then
reduce the oven temperature to moderately hot 180°C
(350°F/Gas 4) and bake for a further 25–30 minutes, or
until golden brown and hollow sounding when tapped
on the base. Remove from the tray and cool on a wire
rack. Serve with butter and eat the same day.

Corn bread

*A quick bread in which cornmeal replaces some
of the flour to produce a slightly grainy, densely
textured bread.*

Preparation time **10 minutes**
Total cooking time **20 minutes**
Makes 1 x 300 g (10 oz) loaf

2 eggs, beaten
250 ml (8 fl oz) buttermilk
60 g (2 oz) butter, melted
185 g (6 oz) fine cornmeal
30 g (1 oz) sugar
60 g (2 oz) self-raising flour
1/4 teaspoon bicarbonate of soda
1 teaspoon salt
2 teaspoons caraway or onion seeds, optional

1 Preheat the oven to moderately hot 190°C (375°F/
Gas 5). Butter a 20 cm (8 inch) square cake tin and dust
with flour, tapping out the excess.
2 Mix the eggs, buttermilk and melted butter together
in a bowl. In another bowl, mix the cornmeal, sugar,
self-raising flour, bicarbonate of soda, salt and caraway
or onion seeds, if using. Pour the buttermilk mixture
into the dry ingredients and beat well with a wooden
spoon until it becomes a smooth batter, then pour into
the prepared tin.
3 Bake the corn bread for 15–20 minutes, or until pale
golden and a skewer inserted into the centre comes out
clean. Cool in the tin for 10 minutes before turning out
onto a wire rack to cool. Serve warm with butter.

Chef's tip Alternatively, the corn bread can be made in
ten well-oiled corn-shaped tins or scalloped madeleine
tins. Bake for about 10–15 minutes before serving as
corn dabs.

Damper (top) and Corn bread

Pumpkin and cardamom rolls

These rolls are a golden orange in colour and their texture is crunchy with pumpkin seeds. Great with butter and honey or as an accompaniment to a bowl of winter vegetable soup.

Preparation time **25 minutes + proving time (about 2 hours)**
Total cooking time **15 minutes**
Makes 12 x 60 g (2 oz) rolls

30 g (1 oz) fresh yeast or 1 tablespoon dried yeast
500 g (1 lb) white bread flour
15 g (¹/2 oz) milk powder
1 teaspoon salt
2 teaspoons ground cardamom
15 g (¹/2 oz) molasses
30 g (1 oz) butter, softened
185 g (6 oz) fresh or tinned pumpkin purée (see Chef's tip)
60 g (2 oz) pumpkin seeds
beaten egg yolk, to glaze

1 Prepare the yeast with 250 ml (8 fl oz) water following the method in the Chef's techniques on page 62.

2 Sieve the flour, milk powder, salt and ground cardamom into a large mixing bowl and make a well in the centre. Stir the molasses into the yeast mixture and add the mixture to the well along with the butter and pumpkin purée. Gradually bring the mixture together with your hands, or use an electric mixer fitted with a dough hook on slow speed, until a fairly soft dough is formed (depending on the moisture content of the pumpkin purée used, you may need to add a little additional flour). Turn the dough out onto a lightly floured work surface and knead for about 10 minutes, or until smooth and elastic (see Chef's techniques, page 62). Alternatively, knead in an electric mixer on medium speed for about 5 minutes.

3 Return the dough to a clean, lightly oiled bowl and turn once to coat the surface in oil. Cover with a clean, damp tea towel and allow to prove at room temperature until doubled in size (the proving time will depend on the temperature of your kitchen).

4 Turn the dough out onto a lightly floured work surface, add the pumpkin seeds and knead for about 3–4 minutes until the dough is smooth and the pumpkin seeds have been distributed evenly without breaking them up. Divide the dough into twelve equal-sized pieces. Using your flat palms, roll each piece on a lightly floured work surface into a 20 cm (8 inch) length and tie in a loose knot, tucking the ends underneath. Butter a baking tray and lift the rolls onto the tray. Cover with a damp tea towel and allow to rise again until nearly doubled in size. Towards the end of this time, preheat the oven to hot 220°C (425°F/Gas 7).

5 Mix the beaten yolk with a tablespoon of water and a pinch of sugar and salt, then gently brush over the proved rolls. Bake for 10–15 minutes, or until golden brown and hollow sounding when tapped on the base. Remove from the tray and cool on a wire rack.

Chef's tip To make the pumpkin purée yourself, steam or boil 200 g (6¹/2 oz) peeled and cubed pumpkin until tender. Mash with a potato masher or purée the pumpkin in a food processor.

Rosetta rolls

A crisp and slightly sweet white roll, with a characteristic flower or pinwheel shape. Split open and fill for light sandwiches.

*Preparation time **25 minutes + proving**
    (about 3 hours 30 minutes)*
*Total cooking time **15 minutes***
Makes 12 x 75 g (2¹/2 oz) rolls

20 g (³/4 oz) fresh yeast or 3 teaspoons dried yeast
30 g (1 oz) caster sugar
600 g (1¹/4 lb) white bread flour
¹/2 teaspoon salt
60 g (2 oz) butter, softened
60 ml (2 fl oz) olive oil
milk, to glaze

1 Prepare the yeast with 300 ml (10 fl oz) water and the sugar following the method in the Chef's techniques on page 62.

2 Sieve the flour and salt into a large mixing bowl and make a well in the centre. Add the yeast mixture, butter and oil to the well and gradually bring the mixture together with your hands, or use an electric mixer fitted with a dough hook on slow speed, until a rough dough is formed. Turn the dough out onto a lightly floured work surface and knead for about 10 minutes, or until smooth and elastic (see Chef's techniques, page 62).

Alternatively, knead in an electric mixer on medium speed for about 5 minutes.

3 Return the dough to a clean, lightly oiled bowl and turn once to coat the surface in oil. Cover with a clean, damp tea towel and allow to prove at room temperature until doubled in size (the proving time will depend on the temperature of your kitchen).

4 Turn the dough out onto a lightly floured work surface and knead gently for 2–3 minutes until smooth. Divide the dough into twelve equal-sized pieces and roll each piece on a lightly floured work surface into a smooth, slightly flattened ball. To give the dough its flower shape, use scissors to snip five cuts about 1 cm (¹/2 inch) deep around the side of each roll. Butter a baking tray, lift the rolls onto the tray, allowing plenty of space between each, and use a 3 cm (1¹/4 inch) pastry cutter to press a centre into each flower to open the petal cuts in the sides slightly. Cover with a damp tea towel and allow to rise again until nearly doubled in size. Towards the end of this time, preheat the oven to hot 210°C (415°F/Gas 6–7).

5 Brush the proved rolls with the milk and bake for 10–15 minutes, or until golden brown and hollow sounding when tapped on the base. Remove from the tray and cool on a wire rack.

This bread doesn't rise ~~much~~ so once put in oven, so shape into a nice round loaf.

+ honey

+ bio yog

Rye bread

Rye is grown in the cool areas of northern and eastern Europe and Scandinavia, and makes a distinctively dense, slightly bitter flavoured bread.

Preparation time **30 minutes + proving (about 4 hours)**
Total cooking time **20 minutes**
Makes **2 x 410 g (13 oz) loaves**

✳ ✳

30 g (1 oz) fresh yeast or 1 tablespoon dried yeast
1 teaspoon caster sugar
300 g (10 oz) white bread flour
250 g (8 oz) rye flour
1 teaspoon salt
15 g (½ oz) milk powder → milk
15 g (½ oz) butter, softened

1 Prepare the yeast with 300 ml (10 fl oz) water and the sugar following the method in the Chef's techniques on page 62.

2 Sieve the flours and salt into a large mixing bowl, stir in the milk powder and make a well in the centre. Add the yeast mixture and butter to the well and gradually bring the mixture together with your hands, or use an electric mixer fitted with a dough hook on slow speed, until a rough dough is formed. Turn the dough out onto a lightly floured work surface and knead for about 10 minutes, or until smooth and elastic (see Chef's techniques, page 62). Alternatively, knead in an electric mixer on medium speed for about 5 minutes.

3 Return the dough to a clean, lightly oiled bowl and turn once to coat the surface in oil. Cover with a clean, damp tea towel and allow to prove at room temperature until doubled in size (the proving time will depend on the temperature of your kitchen).

4 Turn the dough out onto a lightly floured work surface, divide in half and knead gently for 2–3 minutes until smooth. Dust two baking trays with flour. Shape the two pieces of dough into round loaves and lift onto the trays. Use a very sharp knife to cut diagonal slashes in a crisscross pattern on top of the loaves (see Chef's techniques, page 63). Spray the loaves with a fine mist of water and lightly dust the tops with flour. Cover with a damp tea towel and allow to rise again until nearly doubled in size. Towards the end of this time, preheat the oven to moderately hot 200°C (400°F/Gas 6) and place a tin of hot water in the bottom of the oven to produce steam that will help form a crust on the bread.

5 Bake the proved loaves for 20 minutes, or until browned and hollow sounding when tapped on the base. Remove from the trays and cool on a wire rack.

Seeded rolls

These small, soft cloverleaf rolls are made with malted wheat flakes, sunflower, millet, sesame and poppy seeds for a nutty texture.

Preparation time **25 minutes + proving time (about 3 hours)**
Total cooking time **20 minutes**
Makes **12 x 100 g (3¹/₄ oz) rolls**

30 g (1 oz) fresh yeast or 1 tablespoon dried yeast
1 teaspoon sugar
600 g (1¹/₄ lb) white bread flour
2 teaspoons salt
20 g (³/₄ oz) milk powder
45 g (1¹/₂ oz) malted wheat flakes
20 g (³/₄ oz) sunflower seeds
30 g (1 oz) millet seeds
30 g (1 oz) sesame seeds
15 g (¹/₂ oz) poppy seeds
extra poppy seeds, to decorate

1 Prepare the yeast with 470 ml (15 fl oz) water and the sugar following the method in the Chef's techniques on page 62.

2 Sieve the flour and salt into a large mixing bowl, then stir in the milk powder, wheat flakes, sunflower, millet, sesame and poppy seeds. Make a well in the centre and add the yeast mixture to the well. Using your hand with fingers slightly apart, gradually draw the flour into the liquid. Continue until all the flour has been incorporated and a wet, soft dough is formed. Using a wooden spoon or an electric mixer, beat for 3–4 minutes. The dough will seem wet, but the wheat flakes and seeds will absorb moisture during the proving and baking.

3 Return the dough to a clean, lightly oiled bowl and turn once to coat the surface in oil. Cover with a clean, damp tea towel and allow to prove at room temperature until doubled in size (the proving time will depend on the temperature of your kitchen).

4 Turn the dough out onto a lightly floured work surface and knead for about 10 minutes until smooth and elastic (see Chef's techniques, page 62). Butter two 6-hole (250 ml/8 fl oz) muffin tins and dust with flour. Divide the dough into thirty-six pieces and roll on a lightly floured work surface into balls. Tuck three balls side-by-side into each muffin tin hole. Cover with a damp tea towel and allow to rise again until nearly doubled in size. Towards the end of this time, preheat the oven to moderately hot 200°C (400°F/Gas 6).

5 Spray the proved rolls with a fine mist of water, sprinkle on some extra poppy seeds and bake for 15–20 minutes, or until golden. Remove from the oven and cover immediately with clean dry tea towels to cool (this allows the rolls to cool slowly in the steam, resulting in a soft crust and centre).

Rustic loaf

Warm from the oven and with the wholesome taste of honey, grains and natural flours, this bread is great for a ploughman's lunch or to serve with charcuterie or antipasti.

Preparation time **20 minutes + proving time**
  (about 3 hours)
Total cooking time **45 minutes**
Makes **2 x 600 g (1¼ lb) loaves**

30 g (1 oz) brown rice
30 g (1 oz) fresh yeast or 1 tablespoon dried yeast
1 tablespoon honey
315 ml (10 fl oz) buttermilk
2 tablespoons extra virgin olive oil
1 tablespoon salt
75 g (2½ oz) polenta
60 g (2 oz) rolled oats
250 g (8 oz) wholemeal flour
3 tablespoons wheat bran
500 g (1 lb) white bread flour

1 Cook the rice until tender, then drain well and cool.
2 Prepare the yeast with 250 ml (8 fl oz) water following the method in the Chef's techniques on page 62, then stir in the honey.
3 Place the buttermilk, olive oil, salt, rice, polenta, rolled oats, wholemeal flour and wheat bran into a large mixing bowl with 125 g (4 oz) of the white flour. Beat with a wooden spoon or the paddle attachment of an electric mixer until thoroughly combined. Pour in the yeast mixture and beat for 1 minute. Add the remaining flour in four additions, beating well between each, until a soft dough is formed. Turn the dough out onto a lightly floured work surface and knead for about 10 minutes, or until smooth and elastic, although the dough should be very slightly sticky to touch (see Chef's techniques, page 62).
4 Return the dough to a clean, lightly oiled bowl and turn once to coat the surface in oil. Cover with a clean, damp tea towel and allow to prove at room temperature until doubled in size (the proving time will depend on the temperature of your kitchen).
5 Turn the dough out onto a lightly floured work surface, divide in half and knead gently for 2–3 minutes until smooth. Shape the two pieces of dough into round loaves and use a very sharp knife to cut a few slashes in the top of each loaf (see Chef's techniques, page 63). Dust with flour if desired. Butter a large baking tray and place the loaves well apart on the tray. Cover with a damp tea towel and allow to rise again until nearly doubled in size. Towards the end of this time, preheat the oven to moderately hot 190°C (375°F/Gas 5).
6 Bake the proved loaves for 40–45 minutes, or until golden brown and crusty. Remove from the tray and cool on a wire rack.

Coconut roti

A delicious and subtly flavoured flatbread, roti are rolled out on banana leaves in Sri Lanka and can be either sweet or savoury.

Preparation time **55 minutes + 30 minutes standing**
Total cooking time **30 minutes**
Makes 12 x 20 cm (8 inch) roti

250 g (8 oz) fine rice flour
250 g (8 oz) self-raising flour
90 g (3 oz) desiccated coconut
2 teaspoons salt
1/2 teaspoon chilli powder
30 g (1 oz) butter, melted
30 g (1 oz) spring onions, finely chopped
2 tablespoons fresh coriander, finely chopped
1 egg, beaten
vegetable oil, for frying

1 In a large mixing bowl, combine the rice and self-raising flours, desiccated coconut, salt, chilli powder and some black pepper. Place the melted butter in a small bowl and stir in the spring onions and coriander until they are well coated with butter, then add this to the flour mixture. Using a round-bladed knife, evenly distribute the butter mixture through the flour and make a well in the centre.

2 Stir the egg and up to 325 ml (10 1/2 fl oz) lukewarm water (you may need a little less) into the flour to make a fairly stiff dough and mix with your hands until a rough ball has formed. Turn the dough out onto a lightly floured work surface and knead gently for 2–3 minutes until smooth (see Chef's techniques, page 62). Divide the dough into twelve equal-sized pieces. Cover with a damp tea towel and leave to stand at room temperature for about 30 minutes.

3 Roll each piece of dough on a lightly floured work surface into circles about 20 cm (8 inches) across, stacking them lightly while you work. Heat a heavy griddle or frying pan over medium heat, add a little oil and fry a roti until brown flecks appear on the bottom, then turn over and cook the second side. Place on a plate, cover with foil and keep warm while you cook the remaining roti. Serve with chutneys as part of an Asian meal or use like pita bread to wrap up spiced minced meat and salad.

Chef's tips To make almond roti, place whole almonds on a baking tray and roast in a moderate 180°C (350°F/Gas 4) oven for 1–2 minutes, or until golden brown. Process in a food processor to a coarse powder, then use instead of the coconut in the recipe.

For sweet coconut roti, omit the spring onion, coriander and chilli powder and replace instead with 1/2 teaspoon mixed spice and 30 g (1 oz) sultanas.

Country sourdough

Prolonged yeast fermentation gives the characteristic flavour to this sourdough loaf. The starter needs to begin fermenting about two days before the loaf is made.

*Preparation time **30 minutes + proving***
  (2 days in advance for starter and
  3 hours 30 minutes for rising)
*Total cooking time **55 minutes***
*Makes **2 x 500 g (1 lb) loaves***

STARTER
125 g (4 oz) white bread flour
1 teaspoon fresh yeast or 1/2 teaspoon dried yeast
250 ml (8 fl oz) buttermilk or beer

SPONGE
1 teaspoon fresh yeast or 1/2 teaspoon dried yeast
125 g (4 oz) white bread flour

2 teaspoons fresh yeast or 1 teaspoon dried yeast
1 teaspoon salt
2 teaspoons sugar
60 g (2 oz) butter, softened
650 g (1 lb 5 oz) white bread flour
beaten egg, to glaze

1 To make the starter, begin two days before you want to make the bread. Sieve the flour into a large bowl and crumble the yeast over the surface. Heat the buttermilk or beer until lukewarm and mix into the flour using a wooden spoon until a smooth batter is formed. Cover and leave for about 8–12 hours at room temperature, or until the starter begins minutely bubbling.

2 Next, prepare the sponge. Add the yeast and 250 ml (8 fl oz) lukewarm water to the starter and beat with a wooden spoon until the yeast has dissolved. Stir in the flour until smooth, scrape down the sides of the bowl, cover and leave at room temperature for 8–12 hours.

3 On the day you want to bake the bread, place the fermenting starter into a large mixing bowl or the bowl of an electric mixer fitted with a dough hook. Add the last amount of yeast, the salt, sugar, butter and a quarter of the flour, and beat until a smooth paste is formed. Add the remaining flour in three stages, beating well between additions. You should have a soft dough. Turn the dough out onto a lightly floured work surface and knead for about 10 minutes, or until smooth and elastic (see Chef's techniques, page 62).

4 Return the dough to a clean, lightly oiled bowl and turn once to coat the surface in oil. Cover with a clean, damp tea towel and allow to prove at room temperature until doubled in size (the proving time will depend on the temperature of your kitchen).

5 Turn the dough out onto a lightly floured work surface, divide in half and knead gently for about 5 minutes until smooth. Shape the two pieces of dough into round loaves. Dust a baking tray with flour, lift the loaves onto the tray and brush with the beaten egg. Use a very sharp knife to cut a pattern on the top of the loaves like spokes on a wheel (see Chef's techniques, page 63). Cover with a damp tea towel and allow to rise again until nearly doubled in size. Towards the end of this time, preheat the oven to moderately hot 190°C (375°F/Gas 5).

6 Bake the proved loaves for 45–50 minutes, or until deep golden with a good crust. Remove from the tray and cool on a wire rack.

Soft bagels

These yeasted bread rolls, characteristic of Jewish baking, are delicious served warm with butter or filled with cream cheese, smoked salmon and capers. The traditional shiny, hard crust is achieved by boiling the bagels before baking them. Eat within one day.

Preparation time **40 minutes + proving**
 (about 3 hours)
Total cooking time **20 minutes**
Makes 10 bagels

15 g (¹/2 oz) fresh yeast or 2 teaspoons dried yeast
125 ml (4 fl oz) milk
1 teaspoon sugar
450 g (14¹/4 oz) white bread flour
2 teaspoons salt
1 egg, separated
40 g (1¹/4 oz) butter, softened
2 tablespoons dried onions, optional

1 Prepare the yeast with 100 ml (3¹/4 fl oz) water, the milk and the sugar following the method in the Chef's techniques on page 62.

2 Sieve the flour and salt into a large mixing bowl and make a well in the centre. Lightly beat the egg white and add to the well with the yeast mixture and butter. Gradually bring the mixture together with your hands, or use an electric mixer fitted with a dough hook on slow speed, until a soft dough is formed. Turn the dough out onto a lightly floured work surface and knead for about 10 minutes, or until smooth and elastic (see Chef's techniques, page 62). Alternatively, knead in an electric mixer on medium speed for about 5 minutes.

3 Return the dough to a clean, lightly oiled bowl and turn once to coat the surface in oil. Cover with a clean, damp tea towel and allow to prove at room temperature until doubled in size (the proving time will depend on the temperature of your kitchen).

4 Turn the dough out onto a lightly floured work surface and knead gently for 2–3 minutes until smooth. Divide the dough into ten equal-sized pieces and roll each piece on a lightly floured work surface into a tight ball. Poke a finger through the centre and gently enlarge the hole until the ball resembles a doughnut. Butter two baking trays and cut out ten 15 cm (6 inch) square pieces of greaseproof paper, place one under each bagel and lift the bagels onto the trays, allowing plenty of space between them. Cover with a damp tea towel and allow to rise again until nearly doubled in size.

5 Preheat the oven to moderately hot 200°C (400°F/ Gas 6). Bring a large pan of water to the boil, then reduce the heat to simmering. Using a slotted spoon, lower each bagel, still on its square of paper, into the water. Poach for about 30 seconds (the paper will automatically peel off in the water, after which you can discard it). Drain briefly on a tea towel and return to the baking trays.

6 If using the dried onions, pour two tablespoons of boiling water over them and set aside for a few minutes to soften. Mix 1 tablespoon of cold water with the egg yolk and brush the mixture over the surface of the bagels. Squeeze the excess water gently out of the onions and sprinkle these lightly over the bagels. Bake the bagels for 10–15 minutes, or until pale golden. Remove from the trays and cool on a wire rack.

Pretzels

A traditional yeasted, biscuity bread, shaped into loose knots, sprinkled with rock salt and baked to produce a soft, chewy texture. Serve as a snack to go with beer or wine.

Preparation time **30 minutes + proving**
   (about 3 hours 30 minutes)
Total cooking time **25 minutes**
Makes 16 pretzels

25 g (³/4 oz) fresh yeast or 3¹/2 teaspoons dried yeast
250 ml (8 fl oz) milk
600 g (1¹/4 lb) white bread flour
2 tablespoons salt
3 eggs
30 g (1 oz) rock salt

1 Prepare the yeast with the milk following the method in the Chef's techniques on page 62.

2 Sieve the flour and 1 teaspoon of the salt into a large mixing bowl and make a well in the centre. Add the yeast mixture and two of the eggs to the well and whisk with a fork for a few seconds to break up the eggs. Gradually bring the mixture together with your hands, or use an electric mixer fitted with a dough hook on slow speed, until a rough dough is formed. Turn the dough out onto a lightly floured work surface and knead for about 10 minutes, or until smooth and elastic (see Chef's techniques, page 62). Alternatively, knead in an electric mixer on medium speed for about 5 minutes.

3 Return the dough to a clean, lightly oiled bowl and turn once to coat the surface in oil. Cover with a clean, damp tea towel and allow to prove at room temperature until doubled in size (the proving time will depend on the temperature of your kitchen).

4 Turn the dough out onto a lightly floured work surface and knead gently for 2–3 minutes until smooth. Divide the dough into sixteen equal-sized pieces and roll each piece on a lightly floured work surface into 35 cm (14 inch) long sausages, covering the dough with a damp cloth while you work to prevent it from drying out. Tie each sausage into a loose knot, leaving a large hole in the centre. Butter two baking trays and cut out sixteen 15 cm (6 inch) square pieces of greaseproof paper, place one under each pretzel and lift the pretzels onto the trays, allowing plenty of space between them. Cover with a damp tea towel and allow to rise again until nearly doubled in size.

5 Preheat the oven to moderately hot 200°C (400°F/ Gas 6). Bring a large pan of water to the boil with the remaining salt (not the rock salt), then reduce the heat to simmering. Using a slotted spoon, lower the pretzels a few at a time, still on their squares of paper, into the water, being careful not to knock air out of the delicate dough. Poach for about 1 minute per batch (the paper will automatically peel off in the water, after which you can discard it). Drain on paper towels and return to the baking trays.

6 Beat the remaining egg and brush over the surface of the pretzels. Gently press the rock salt onto the surface of the pretzels and bake for 10–15 minutes, or until pale golden. Remove fom the trays and cool on a wire rack.

Soda bread

A traditional Irish bread made with bicarbonate of soda instead of yeast and with buttermilk adding extra richness.

Preparation time **10 minutes**
Total cooking time **40 minutes**
Makes 1 x 800 g (1lb 10 oz) loaf

500 g (1 lb) white bread flour
2 teaspoons bicarbonate of soda
2 teaspoons cream of tartar
1/2 teaspoon salt
2 teaspoons caster sugar
30 g (1 oz) butter or lard, cubed and chilled
250 ml (8 fl oz) buttermilk
1 tablespoon milk

1 Preheat the oven to a moderately hot 200°C (400°F/ Gas 6). Sieve the flour, bicarbonate of soda, cream of tartar, salt and sugar into a large mixing bowl. Tip the mixture onto a sheet of greaseproof paper, then sieve again into the bowl (this ensures the raising agents and flour are evenly mixed and helps to incorporate air).
2 Rub the butter or lard into the flour using a light, flicking action of thumbs across fingertips until the mixture resembles fine breadcrumbs. Make a well in the centre, add the buttermilk and milk to the well and gradually bring the mixture together with your hands until a soft dough is formed. Add a little more milk if your dough is dry. Turn the dough out onto a lightly floured work surface and knead for about 10 minutes, or until smooth and elastic (see Chef's techniques, page 62).
3 Flour a baking tray, shape the dough into a slightly flattened round and lift onto the tray. Use a very sharp knife to cut a wide cross on the top of the loaf, about 2 cm (3/4 inch) deep (see Chef's techniques, page 63) and bake immediately for 30–40 minutes. Remove from the tray and cool on a wire rack.

Herby cheese rolls

These rolls combine the gutsy flavour of goat's cheese with fresh chives, marjoram, oregano and thyme.

Preparation time **15 minutes**
Total cooking time **25 minutes**
Makes 12 rolls

450 g (14 1/4 oz) self-raising flour
3 teaspoons salt
60 g (2 oz) butter, cubed and chilled
2 tablespoons fresh chives, chopped
2 tablespoons fresh marjoram, chopped
1 tablespoon fresh oregano, chopped
1 tablespoon fresh thyme leaves
200 g (6 1/2 oz) goat's cheese, crumbled
2 eggs, beaten

1 Preheat the oven to moderate 180°C (350°F/Gas 4). Butter and flour a 12-hole (125 ml/4 fl oz capacity) muffin tin.
2 Sieve the flour and salt into a large mixing bowl and rub in the butter using a light, flicking action of thumbs across fingertips until the mixture resembles fine breadcrumbs. Stir in the chives, marjoram, oregano, thyme and goat's cheese, then season the mixture with a generous amount of black pepper.
3 Zigzag the beaten egg across the top of the flour mixture and roughly fork through before adding 300 ml (10 fl oz) water. Stir until everything is just blended and spoon into the muffin tins.
4 Bake for 20–25 minutes, or until golden brown and hollow sounding when tapped on the base. Turn out of the tin and cool on a wire rack.

Chef's tip A little extra cheese can be sprinkled over the top of the rolls 15 minutes after placing in the oven. Use about 60 g (2 oz) goat's cheese or a mild, coloured cheese such as Red Leicester.

Soda bread (top) and Herby cheese rolls

Challah

An impressive four-strand plaited loaf, traditionally made as a Jewish Sabbath offering, with a light, creamy inside and a rich flavour.

*Preparation time **20 minutes + proving**
 (about 2 hours 45 minutes)*
*Total cooking time **40 minutes***
Makes 1 x 1.3 kg (2 lb 10 oz) loaf

❁ ❁ ❁

30 g (1 oz) fresh yeast or 1 tablespoon dried yeast
1 tablespoon sugar
750 g (1 1/2 lb) white bread flour
1 teaspoon salt
90 g (3 oz) butter, softened
3 eggs, beaten
2 beaten egg yolks, to glaze
1–2 tablespoons poppy seeds

1 Prepare the yeast with 90 ml (3 fl oz) water and 1 teaspoon of the sugar following the method in the Chef's techniques on page 62.

2 Sieve the flour and salt into a large mixing bowl and make a well in the centre. Add the yeast mixture, the remaining sugar, butter, eggs and about 250 ml (8 fl oz) lukewarm water to the well. Using your hand with fingers slightly apart, gradually draw the flour into the liquid. Continue until all the flour has been incorporated and the dough comes together to form a soft ball. The dough should be soft and hold its shape without being sticky (you may need to add a little more flour or water). Turn the dough out onto a lightly floured work surface and knead for about 10 minutes, or until smooth and elastic (see Chef's techniques, page 62). Alternatively, knead in an electric mixer on medium speed for about 5 minutes.

3 Return the dough to a clean, lightly oiled bowl and turn once to coat the surface in oil. Cover with a clean, damp tea towel and allow to prove at room temperature until doubled in size (the proving time will depend on the temperature of your kitchen).

4 Turn the dough out onto a lightly floured work surface and knead for 1 minute. Cover with a clean, damp tea towel and set aside for 5 minutes, then divide the dough into four pieces. Roll each piece on a lightly floured work surface into 50 cm (20 inch) long sausages. Pinch the four strands together firmly at one end and place on the work surface in front of you with the join at the top. Starting with the left outside strand, take it under the two middle strands and then back over the top of the nearest one. Repeat with the outside right strand. Continue this sequence until the loaf has been plaited all the way to the bottom, then seal the ends firmly and neatly.

5 Butter a baking tray and lift the plait onto the tray. Cover with a damp tea towel and allow to rise again until nearly doubled in size. Towards the end of this time, preheat the oven to hot 220°C (425°F/Gas 7).

6 Mix a tablespoon of water with the egg yolks and brush the proved loaf with half the mixture. Bake for 10 minutes, then brush again with the yolk and sprinkle liberally with the poppy seeds. Return to the oven and bake, covering the top with foil if the loaf starts to brown too much, for a further 25–30 minutes, or until hollow sounding when tapped on the base. Remove from the tray and cool on a wire rack.

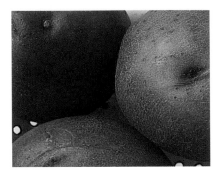

Potato bread

A pale, moist and soft textured bread made with flour, oatmeal and potato. The dark crust is produced by the unusual glaze of natural yoghurt.

*Preparation time **25 minutes + proving time**
 (about 2 hours 30 minutes)*
*Total cooking time **1 hour***
*Makes **2 x 650 g (1 lb 5 oz) loaves***

I large potato (about 250 g/8 oz), cut into cubes
30 g (I oz) fresh yeast or I tablespoon dried yeast
I tablespoon sugar
40 g (I¼ oz) butter, melted
I teaspoon salt
650 g (I lb 5 oz) white bread flour
155 g (5 oz) coarse oatmeal
315 ml (10 fl oz) milk, lukewarm
2 tablespoons natural yoghurt, to glaze

1 Place the potato in a pan, cover with water and bring to the boil. Reduce the heat and simmer for 15 minutes, or until tender. Drain, reserving 125 ml (4 fl oz) of the water (set aside to cool to lukewarm). Mash the potato until very smooth using a food mill or sieve.

2 Prepare the yeast with the lukewarm potato water and a pinch of the sugar following the method in the Chef's techniques on page 62.

3 Place the yeast in a large mixing bowl or in the bowl of an electric mixer fitted with a paddle attachment.

Add the remaining sugar, potato, butter and salt and beat just until smooth. Add the flour, oatmeal and milk and mix until a soft dough is formed. The dough will seem sticky, but the oatmeal will absorb moisture during the proving and baking. Turn the dough out onto a lightly floured work surface and knead for 2–3 minutes, or until elastic (see Chef's techniques, page 62).

4 Return the dough to a clean, lightly oiled bowl and turn once to coat the surface in oil. Cover with a clean, damp tea towel and allow to prove at room temperature until doubled in size (the proving time will depend on the temperature of your kitchen).

5 Turn the dough out onto a lightly floured work surface, divide in half and knead gently for 2–3 minutes until smooth. Shape the two pieces of dough into round loaves. Butter two 20 cm (8 inch) round tins, dust with flour and lift the loaves into the tins. Cover with a damp tea towel and allow to rise again until nearly doubled in size. Towards the end of this time, preheat the oven to moderately hot 200°C (400°F/Gas 6).

6 Bake the proved loaves for 25–30 minutes, then reduce the oven temperature to moderate 180°C (350°F/Gas 4). Turn out of the tins and brush the tops with yoghurt. Return to the oven on a tray for 10–15 minutes, or until deep golden and hollow sounding when tapped on the base. Remove from the tray and cool on a wire rack.

Beer bread

For maximum flavour with minimum effort, it is difficult to beat this rustic bread. Eat for lunch with some leg ham and English mustard.

Preparation time **15 minutes**
Total cooking time **40 minutes**
Makes 1 x 1 kg (2 lb) loaf

250 g (8 oz) plain flour
250 g (8 oz) stoneground wholemeal flour
1 1/2 teaspoons bicarbonate of soda
1/2 teaspoon salt
1 tablespoon clear honey
375 ml (12 fl oz) malty brown ale

1 Preheat the oven to moderately hot 190°C (375°F/ Gas 5). Sieve the flours, bicarbonate of soda and salt together into a large mixing bowl, then stir in the honey and ale to make a heavy wet dough.
2 Butter a 1 kg (2 lb) loaf tin and dust the inside with some flour, tapping out the excess. Spoon the mixture into the tin and smooth the surface with the back of a wet spoon.
3 Bake for 35–40 minutes, or until the loaf is golden brown and a skewer inserted into the centre comes out clean. Remove from the tin and cool on a wire rack.

Chef's tip For a variation, add 60 g (2 oz) finely chopped, cooked French shallots with the honey.

Pain aux lardons

A quick bread with an enticingly savoury combination of crispy bacon and onions. Serve plain or with butter.

Preparation time **20 minutes**
Total cooking time **50 minutes**
Makes 1 x 1 kg (2 lb) loaf

375 g (12 oz) self-raising flour
1 teaspoon black pepper
185 g (6 oz) butter, cubed and chilled
155 g (5 oz) speck or rindless streaky bacon, diced
90 g (3 oz) French shallots, finely diced
4 eggs, beaten
2 tablespoons milk

1 Preheat the oven to moderate 180°C (350°F/Gas 4). Sieve the flour, pepper and a generous pinch of salt into a large mixing bowl. Add the butter and rub into the flour using a light, flicking action of thumbs across fingertips until the mixture resembles fine breadcrumbs. Make a well in the centre.
2 Put the bacon into a cold frying pan and heat over a low flame until the fat begins to run from it, then raise the heat to medium and fry until crisp. Using a slotted spoon, remove the bacon to a plate and fry the shallots in the same pan until soft and tinged brown around the edges. Stir the bacon, shallots and any remaining fat into the flour mixture along with the beaten eggs and milk, and mix thoroughly to make a stiff dough. Butter a 1 kg (2 lb) loaf tin and line the base with baking paper. Spoon the mixture into the tin and smooth the surface with the back of a wet spoon.
3 Bake for 45–50 minutes, or until a skewer inserted into the centre comes out clean. Leave to cool for about 5 minutes in the tin, then turn out onto a wire rack to cool.

Beer bread (left) and Pain aux lardons

Fougasse

Traditionally eaten in Provence on Christmas Eve as one of thirteen desserts symbolizing Christ and his disciples, each region in France now has its own version of this oldest of French breads.

*Preparation time **40 minutes + proving**
  (about 4 hours)*
*Total cooking time **10 minutes***
Makes 6 x 200 g (6¹/2 oz) rolls

15 g (¹/2 oz) fresh yeast or 2 teaspoons dried yeast
680 g (1 lb 6 oz) white bread flour
1¹/2 teaspoons salt
125 g (4 oz) sugar
3 eggs, beaten
grated rind and juice of 1 large orange
2 tablespoons brandy
90 g (3 oz) butter, softened
90 g (3 oz) high-quality candied peel, chopped
30 g (1 oz) butter, melted
2 tablespoons orange flower water

1 Prepare the yeast with 90 ml (3 fl oz) water following the method in the Chef's techniques on page 62.

2 Sponge the dough by sieving the flour into a large mixing bowl, adding the salt and sugar and following the method in the Chef's techniques on page 63. In a small bowl, mix together the eggs, orange rind and juice and brandy, pour into the well after the yeast has risen and stir to form a soft dough. Add the butter, squeezing and folding it into the dough until fully incorporated. Turn the dough out onto a lightly floured work surface and knead for about 10 minutes, or until smooth and elastic (see Chef's techniques, page 62). Alternatively, knead in an electric mixer on medium speed for about 5 minutes.

3 Return the dough to a clean, lightly oiled bowl and turn once to coat the surface in oil. Cover with a clean, damp tea towel and allow to prove at room temperature until doubled in size (the proving time will depend on the temperature of your kitchen).

4 Turn the dough out onto a lightly floured work surface and gently knead in the candied peel for about 5 minutes, or until the dough is smooth and the peel is evenly distributed. Divide the dough into six equal-sized pieces and roll each one on a lightly floured work surface into a 15 x 20 cm (6 x 8 inch) oval, 1 cm (¹/2 inch) thick. Place the fougasse on a board and use a very sharp knife to cut slashes through to the board, beginning in the centre of one side of the dough and working outwards to give shell-like grooves. Butter two baking trays and lift the fougasse onto the trays, allowing plenty of space between each one. Cover with a damp tea towel and allow to rise again until nearly doubled in size. Towards the end of this time, preheat the oven to moderately hot 200°C (400°F/Gas 6).

5 Brush the proved fougasse with half the melted butter and bake for 7–10 minutes, or until golden brown. Remove from the oven and, while the bread is still warm, brush with the remaining butter and the orange flower water. Remove from the tray and cool on a wire rack.

Banana bread

A moist, beautifully golden and speedy bread with warm spice flavours. This bread is perfect for afternoon teas and lunch boxes, especially spread with creamy butter.

Preparation time **20 minutes**
Total cooking time **45 minutes**
Makes 2 x 500 g (1 lb) loaves

250 g (8 oz) plain flour
2 teaspoons baking powder
250 g (8 oz) very ripe bananas
250 g (8 oz) soft light brown sugar
1/4 teaspoon freshly grated nutmeg
3 eggs
3 tablespoons vegetable oil
70 ml (21/4 fl oz) milk
2 tablespoons apricot jam
icing sugar, to dust

1 Preheat the oven to warm 160°C (315°F/Gas 2–3).
2 Sieve the flour, baking powder and a pinch of salt into a large mixing bowl. In a smaller bowl, mash the bananas, brown sugar and grated nutmeg with a fork until creamy.
3 Using a wooden spoon, beat the eggs into the banana mixture one at a time, beating well between each one. Stir the banana mixture gently into the dry ingredients, then add the vegetable oil and milk and mix together quickly but thoroughly using the wooden spoon.
4 Butter two 500 g (1 lb) loaf tins and line the bases with baking paper. Pour the mixture into the tins, filling them no more than two-thirds full, and bake for 35–40 minutes, covering with foil if the breads brown too much. After about 15 minutes, when the top has begun to form a skin, use a serrated knife to cut down the centre of the breads to a 1 cm (1/2 inch) depth (this will ensure the breads have an attractive, even-crusted appearance once cooked).
5 Remove the breads from the oven when they are golden and a skewer inserted into the centre of them comes out clean. Leave to cool for 5 minutes in the tin, then turn out onto a wire rack to cool.
6 In a small pan, heat the apricot jam. When the jam has melted and begins to boil, sieve it into a small bowl and, while still hot, brush it over the cooled breads. Sprinkle with some icing sugar just before serving.

Chef's tip This recipe can also be used to make delicious apple or apricot bread. Simply replace the mashed banana with the same amount of chunky apple or apricot compote.

Spicy bread

*An unusual honey and orange-scented loaf that will appeal to those who like their bread light and spicy.
Excellent spread with unsalted butter for afternoon tea.*

Preparation time **15 minutes**
Total cooking time **1 hour 5 minutes**
Makes 1 x 650 g (1 lb 5 oz) loaf

100 g (3¹/4 oz) butter
100 g (3¹/4 oz) sugar
100 ml (3¹/4 fl oz) honey
250 g (8 oz) plain flour
60 g (2 oz) rye flour
2 teaspoons baking powder
I teaspoon ground cinnamon
I teaspoon ground aniseed
¹/2 teaspoon ground ginger
grated rind of I orange

1 Preheat the oven to warm 160°C (315°F/Gas 2–3).
2 Place the butter, sugar, honey and 125 ml (4 fl oz) water in a small pan. Using a wooden spoon, stir over a low heat until the butter has melted and the sugar has dissolved. Remove from the heat and cool slightly.

3 Meanwhile, sieve the flours, baking powder, cinnamon, aniseed, ginger and a pinch of salt into a large bowl and make a well in the centre. Pour the cooled sugar and honey mixture and the orange rind into the dry ingredients and mix thoroughly.

4 Butter a 500 g (1 lb) loaf tin and line the base and sides with baking paper. Pour the mixture into the tin and bake for 1 hour, or until a skewer inserted into the centre of the loaf comes out clean. Remove from the tin and cool on a wire rack. Serve sliced and spread with some butter.

Chef's tip This recipe can also be used to make a spicy date bread. Just add 90 g (3 oz) finely chopped stoned dates with the flours, and proceed as above.

Saffron bread

A traditional Greek festival bread made from honey, raisins and orange and lemon rind, with a rich yellow colour and delicate flavour from the luxurious spice saffron. Wonderful toasted for breakfast.

Preparation time **25 minutes + proving**
   (about 2 hours 30 minutes) + 30 minutes soaking
Total cooking time **35 minutes**
Makes 2 x 600 g (1¼ lb) loaves

1–2 good pinches of saffron threads
30 g (1 oz) fresh yeast or 1 tablespoon dried yeast
2 teaspoons clear honey, preferably Greek
750 g (1½ lb) white bread flour
½ teaspoon salt
grated rind of ½ orange
grated rind of ½ lemon
15 g (½ oz) milk powder
15 g (½ oz) butter, softened
100 g (3¼ oz) raisins
beaten egg yolk, to glaze

1 Place the saffron in a bowl, cover with 2 tablespoons boiling water and stand for 20–30 minutes. Prepare the yeast with 410 ml (13 fl oz) water following the method in the Chef's techniques on page 62, then add the honey.
2 Sieve the flour and salt into a large mixing bowl, stir in the rind and milk powder and make a well in the centre. Add the yeast mixture, butter and saffron and its liquid to the well. Using your hand with fingers slightly

apart, gradually draw the flour into the liquid. Continue until all the flour has been incorporated and a soft dough is formed. Turn the dough out onto a lightly floured work surface and knead for about 10 minutes, gradually adding the raisins, until the dough is smooth and elastic (see Chef's techniques, page 62).
3 Return the dough to a clean, lightly oiled bowl and turn once to cover the surface in oil. Cover with a clean, damp tea towel and allow to prove at room temperature until doubled in size (the proving time will depend on the temperature of your kitchen).
4 Turn the dough out onto a lightly floured work surface and roll into two 20 x 25 cm (8 x 10 inch) rectangles. Spray with a fine mist of water, then roll up tightly into a sausage shape (see Chef's techniques, page 63). Butter and flour two baking trays and lift the bread onto the trays, seam-side-down. Use a very sharp knife to cut five diagonal slashes in the loaves (see Chef's techniques, page 63). Cover with a damp tea towel and allow to rise again until nearly doubled in size. Towards the end of this time, preheat the oven to hot 210° C (415°F/Gas 6–7).
5 Mix the yolk with a pinch of sugar and salt and brush over the proved loaves. Bake for 30–35 minutes, or until golden brown and hollow sounding when tapped on the base. Remove from the trays and cool on a wire rack.

Stollen

This sweet, yeasty German Christmas bread is usually baked several weeks before Christmas to allow the flavour of the spices to mature. When cooked, it is liberally brushed with butter for a delicious crust.

Preparation time **1 hour + proving**
  (about 4 hours) + overnight marinating
Total cooking time **50 minutes**
Makes 2 stollen (each cuts into 16 slices)

1 teaspoon ground mixed spice
155 g (5 oz) chopped mixed peel
45 g (1½ oz) glacé cherries, quartered
60 g (2 oz) flaked almonds
2 tablespoons rum
grated rind of 2 small lemons
155 g (5 oz) raisins
90 ml (3 fl oz) milk
30 g (1 oz) fresh yeast or 1 tablespoon dried yeast
375 g (12 oz) plain flour
55 g (1¾ oz) sugar
185 g (6 oz) butter, cubed and chilled
1 egg, beaten
beaten egg and egg yolk, for glazing
30 g (1 oz) butter, melted
icing sugar, to dust

1 Mix the ground mixed spice, mixed peel, cherries, almonds, rum, lemon rind and raisins together. Cover and marinate overnight.

2 Put the milk in a small pan and heat until tepid. Pour into a bowl and dissolve the yeast in it. Sieve 125 g (4 oz) of the flour and 1½ teaspoons of the sugar into a large mixing bowl and make a well in the centre. Add the yeast mixture to the well and mix to a smooth paste, then cover with plastic wrap and allow to prove at room temperature until doubled in size (the proving time will depend on the temperature of your kitchen).

3 Add the butter to the remaining flour and rub in using a light, flicking action of thumbs across fingertips until the mixture resembles fine breadcrumbs, then stir in the remaining sugar and ½ teaspoon salt. Pour in the beaten egg and mix well.

4 Add the proved yeast mixture to the dough and mix until smooth, then stir in the marinated ingredients. Turn the dough out onto a lightly floured work surface and knead for about 5 minutes, or until smooth and elastic (see Chef's techniques, page 62).

5 Place the dough in a large lightly floured bowl, cover with a clean, damp tea towel and allow to prove at room temperature until doubled in size.

6 Turn the dough out onto a lightly floured work surface, divide in half and knead gently for 2–3 minutes until smooth. Shape the two pieces of dough into 22 x 25 cm (9 x 10 inch) rectangles, then roll into cylinders. Butter two large baking trays and lift the stollen onto the trays, seam-side-down. Cover with a damp tea towel and allow to rise again until nearly doubled in size. Towards the end of this time, preheat the oven to moderate 180°C (350°F/Gas 4).

7 Lightly brush the proved stollen with the beaten egg and egg yolk and bake for 35–45 minutes, or until well risen and golden. Remove from the oven and, while the stollen is still warm, brush with the melted butter and dust liberally with the icing sugar. Remove from the trays and cool on a wire rack.

Chef's tips For a marzipan-filled stollen, roll two 125 g (4 oz) pieces of marzipan into cylinders and roll the stollen dough around them.

This recipe makes two stollen, which is perfect if you are baking for a large Christmas gathering. Otherwise, wrap one in plastic wrap, then aluminium foil, and freeze for up to 3 months.

A stollen makes a lovely Christmas gift, wrapped in cellophane and tied with ribbon.

Hot cross buns

The irresistible aroma of these spiced buns and the appeal of them toasted and buttered means hot cross buns are baked all year round, not just for Easter.

*Preparation time **25 minutes + proving**
  (about 2 hours 30 minutes or overnight)*
*Total cooking time **20 minutes***
Makes 16

30 g (1 oz) fresh yeast or 1 tablespoon dried yeast
180 ml (5³/4 fl oz) milk
500 g (1 lb) white bread flour
2 teaspoons mixed spice
60 g (2 oz) sugar
2 teaspoons salt
2 eggs, beaten
120 g (4 oz) butter, softened
120 g (4 oz) sultanas

TOPPING AND GLAZE
4 tablespoons plain flour
6 tablespoons sugar
4 tablespoons milk
¹/2 teaspoon mixed spice

1 Prepare the yeast with the milk following the method in the Chef's techniques on page 62.
2 Sieve the flour, mixed spice, sugar and salt into a large mixing bowl and make a well in the centre. Add the yeast mixture and egg to the well and gradually bring the mixture together with your hands, or use an electric mixer fitted with a dough hook on slow speed, until a soft dough is formed. Turn the dough out onto a lightly floured work surface and knead for about 10 minutes, or until smooth and elastic (see Chef's techniques, page 62). Knead the softened butter into the dough until it is fully incorporated and the dough is silky and soft.
3 Return the dough to a clean, lightly oiled bowl and turn once to coat the surface in oil. Cover with a clean, damp tea towel and allow to prove at room temperature until doubled in size (the proving time will depend on the temperature of your kitchen) or leave overnight in the refrigerator.
4 Turn the dough out onto a lightly floured work surface and knead in the sultanas until they are just evenly distributed. Divide into sixteen equal-sized pieces and roll each piece on a lightly floured work surface in the hollow of your hand until it forms a round and smooth ball. Butter a baking tray and place the buns slightly apart on the tray. Cover with a damp tea towel and allow to rise again until nearly doubled in size (the buns will be touching when they are ready). Towards the end of this time, preheat the oven to moderately hot 200°C (400°F/Gas 6).
5 To make the topping and glaze, mix together the flour, 4 tablespoons of the sugar and 2–3 tablespoons of water to form a smooth, thick paste. Place in a piping bag fitted with a small plain nozzle and pipe the paste across the proved buns in continuous straight lines so that each bun has a cross on top.
6 Bake the buns for 10–15 minutes, or until golden and hollow sounding when tapped on the base. Meanwhile, heat the milk, remaining sugar and mixed spice in a small pan until the sugar has dissolved. Brush this glaze over the buns as they come out of the oven. Remove from the tray and cool on a wire rack, then brush again with the glaze. Serve plain or split and toasted with some butter.

Panettone

Individually made and wrapped in cellophane and ribbons, this Milanese Christmas speciality is a wonderful gift. High-quality crystallized fruit will taste much better than ready-chopped candied peel.

Preparation time 25 minutes + proving (about
  4 hours or overnight) + 1 hour or overnight soaking
Total cooking time 45 minutes
Makes 6 x 155 g (5 oz) loaves

60 g (2 oz) golden raisins
60 g (2 oz) mixed candied fruits, finely chopped
135 ml (4 1/2 fl oz) Cointreau
1 tablespoon orange flower water
30 g (1 oz) fresh yeast or 1 tablespoon dried yeast
90 g (3 oz) sugar
500 g (1 lb) white bread flour
1 teaspoon mixed spice
1 teaspoon salt
150 ml (5 fl oz) milk, lukewarm
120 g (4 oz) butter, softened
2 eggs, beaten
60 g (2 oz) macadamia nuts, chopped

1 Prepare six tins, about 10 cm (4 inches) high and 7 cm (2 3/4 inches) in diameter (washed baked bean tins are ideal) by brushing with melted butter and lining the base and sides with greaseproof paper. Allow a 4 cm (1 1/2 inch) collar to extend above the rims of the tins. Brush a second time with butter to smooth down the edges of the paper.

2 Place the raisins, candied fruits, Cointreau and orange flower water in a small bowl and leave to soak for at least one hour, or overnight if possible.

3 Prepare the yeast with 2 tablespoons warm water and a pinch of the sugar following the method in the Chef's techniques on page 62.

4 Sieve the flour, mixed spice, salt and all but 2 tablespoons of the remaining sugar into a large mixing bowl and make a well in the centre. Drain the soaked fruits, reserving the Cointreau soaking liquid, and add to the well. Add the warm milk, butter, eggs, nuts and yeast mixture. Gradually bring the mixture together with your hands, or use an electric mixer fitted with a dough hook on slow speed, until a soft dough is formed. Turn the dough out onto a lightly floured work surface and knead for about 10 minutes, or until smooth and elastic (see Chef's techniques, page 62).

5 Return the dough to a clean, lightly oiled bowl and turn once to coat the surface in oil. Cover with a clean, damp tea towel and allow to prove at room temperature until doubled in size (the proving time will depend on the temperature of your kitchen) or leave overnight in the refrigerator.

6 Turn the dough out onto a lightly floured work surface and knead gently for 2–3 minutes. Divide the dough into six equal-sized pieces and roll each piece of dough out on a lightly floured work surface into tight balls. If any fruit or nuts break through the surface of the dough, remove these and press into the base of the balls to stop them burning. Place in the prepared tins, put on a baking tray and cover with a damp tea towel. Allow to rise again until the dough has risen nearly to the top of the tins. Towards the end of this time, preheat the oven to moderate 180°C (350°F/Gas 4).

7 Bake the proved panettone for 30–40 minutes, or until golden brown and hollow sounding when tapped on the base, covering with a piece of foil after the first 15 minutes.

8 Meanwhile, prepare a glaze by topping up the reserved soaking liquid from the fruit with water, if necessary, until you have 60 ml (2 fl oz) liquid. Heat in a pan with the last 2 tablespoons of sugar until the sugar has dissolved completely. Brush the baked panettone twice all over with the glaze while still warm, then remove from their tins and cool on a wire rack. The panettone can be stored in an airtight container for up to one month.

Chef's techniques

◆

Yeast

Yeast is very sensitive, so the water must be hand hot (the same temperature as a finger placed in it).

If using dried yeast, place the water in a small glass bowl and sprinkle the yeast and sugar, if specified in the recipe, over it. Leave to dissolve for 5 minutes, then stir with a wooden spoon.

If using fresh yeast, crumble the yeast into a small glass bowl and add the water and sugar, if specified in the recipe. Cream together, then stir in a pinch of flour. Leave until bubbles form on the surface.

If using easy-blend yeast, sift the yeast into a bowl with all the dry ingredients. The yeast will be activated when the liquid is added.

Kneading

Kneading is very important to distribute the yeast and allow gluten to develop.

Place the dough on a lightly floured work surface and begin to knead it.

Flatten the dough away from you, then fold it over towards you and continue this kneading.

As the dough becomes more stretchy, use the heel of your hand to push one half of the dough away from you as you pull the other half towards you. Rotate the dough as you knead.

The dough is well kneaded when it is smooth, shiny and elastic. A finger mark pressed into the dough should spring back immediately.